BUGS

SIMON TYLER

PAVILION

CONTENTS

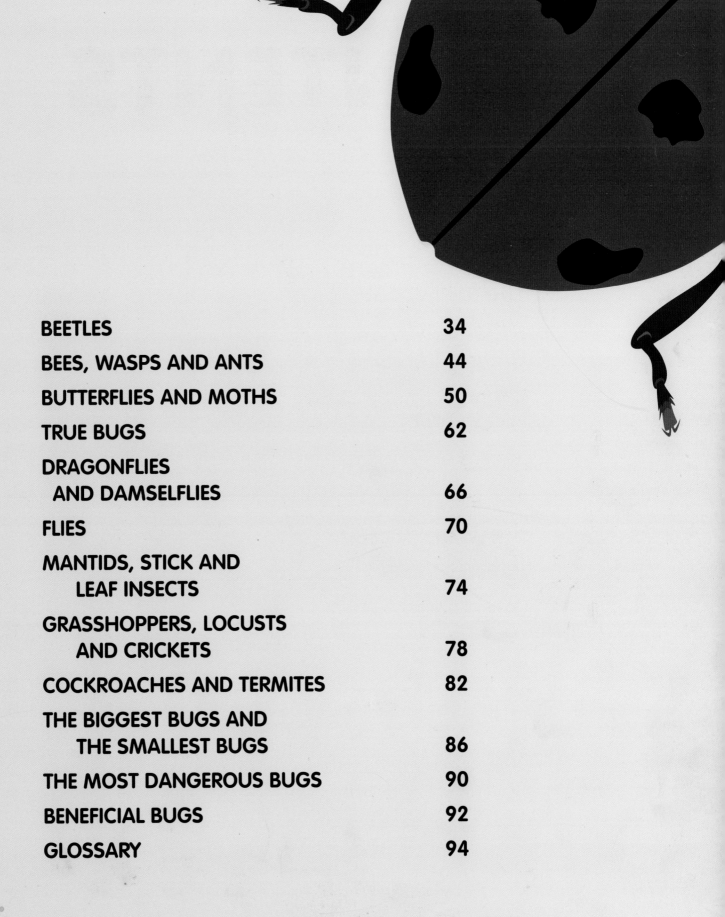

INTRODUCTION

Welcome to the fascinating world of bugs

There are more bugs on our planet than any other type of animal, and still we only know about a small fraction of the number of bug species that are thought to exist. Scientists have described over a million of them, but there are likely to be many, many more out there waiting to be discovered.

Bugs come in a staggering array of body shapes, sizes and colours. Some of them fly, others walk or crawl, some dig and some swim. They live in virtually every environment on Earth, from massive mountains to the deepest jungles, dry deserts to the surface of the oceans — even in high-rise city centres!

The aim of this book is to give you a good understanding of bugs — their behaviour and their variety — and to celebrate the staggering range and beauty of bug life. We start by introducing topics about bugs in general — from what they are to how they live, how they use their senses and how they defend themselves from predators. We then investigate the different types of bug in more detail.

The illustrations aren't to scale. We've shown the insects larger than life so that you can see them in detail, but each is noted with its actual size.

In parts of this book you may find some scientific terms that you are unfamiliar with. The first time these are used, they are highlighted in **BOLD CAPITALS** and all of these words and phrases are explained in the glossary at the end of the book.

Blue fungus beetle
Gibbifer californicus
Length: 15mm

Found in the
southwestern USA
and northern Mexico

This beetle gets its name because of its diet — it likes to feed on rotting fungi.

WHAT ARE BUGS?

In this book we have used the word "bugs" to describe the entire **CLASS** of insects. Strictly speaking, only one section of the insect world is made up of bugs. "Bugs" is the scientific name used to describe members of the **ORDER** *hemiptera* but, because the word is so commonly used to describe insects in general, we have followed the convention of referring to the *hemiptera* as true bugs.

One example of the *hemiptera* order is the **Picasso bug** – *Sphaerocoris annulus* – on the right.

All bugs share certain **CHARACTERISTICS** which place them in the insect class:

1 – They all have six legs, and so are known as **HEXAPODS** (from the Greek *hex* meaning six and *poda* meaning foot or leg).

2 – They all have a hard outer skeleton, called an **EXOSKELETON**.

3 – They all have a three-part body, made up of a **HEAD CAPSULE**, a **THORAX** and an **ABDOMEN**.

Bugs are all part of the larger **ARTHROPOD PHYLUM** (category), which also contains arachnids (such as spiders and scorpions), myriapods (including centipedes and millipedes) and crustaceans (e.g. shrimp, krill, woodlice, crabs and lobsters).

Picasso bug
Sphaerocoris annulus
Length: 8mm

Found across Africa, including Kenya, Tanzania, Nigeria and South Africa

Named after the Spanish artist Pablo Picasso, because of the similarity between the look of his work and its pattern. Like other shield bugs, it can release a squirt of nasty-smelling liquid to scare off potential predators.

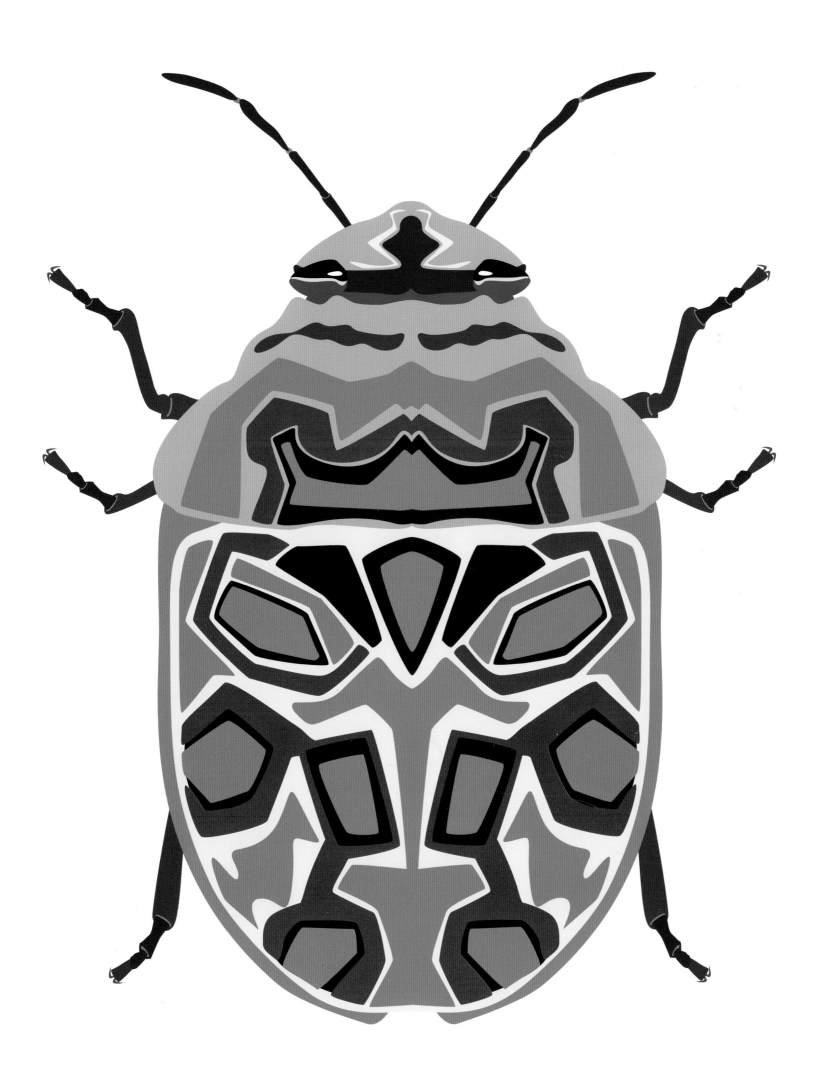

TYPES OF BUG

As we have already learned, insects make up a class of animals. In biology, types of **ORGANISM** are grouped together into sets. This is known as **TAXONOMY**.
The differences between bugs have led scientists to separate them into orders, **FAMILIES** and **SPECIES**.

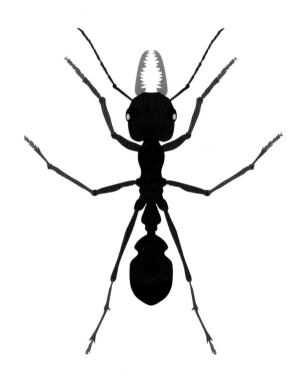

RED BULL ANT

CLASS	GENUS
Insecta	Myrmecia
ORDER	SPECIES
Hymenoptera	*Myrmecia gulosa*
FAMILY	
Formicidae	

For example, consider the red bull ant on the left. The scientific name for this type of ant (known as the **BINOMIAL** name) is *Myrmecia gulosa*.

That name tells us the ant's species. A species is a single type of living organism that breeds to produce **FERTILE** offspring.

The first part of the name – *Myrmecia* – is known as the **GENUS**. The genus is a set that the ant belongs to. Other ants in the same genus will be very similar, but will perhaps have some small differences, such as their shape, size or where they live.

All ants belong to another, bigger set, which is known as the family. The ant family is called *formicidae*. Every type of ant on Earth (living or extinct) belongs to this family. Even ants that haven't been discovered yet form part of this set.

The ant family and other families (including the bee family and wasp families) form an even bigger set, known as an order. In this case, the order is called *hymenoptera*.

The *hymenoptera* order and other orders form an even bigger set, called a class.

As we already know, this is the insect class, known as *insecta*.

The main insect orders are:

Blattodea
Cockroaches
and termites

Coleoptera
Beetles

Diptera
Flies

Hemiptera
True bugs

Hymenoptera
Bees, wasps
and ants

Lepidoptera
Butterflies
and moths

Mantodea
Mantids

Orthoptera
Grasshoppers
and crickets

Odonata
Dragonflies
and damselflies

Phasmatodea
Stick insects
and leaf insects

THE BUG LIFE CYCLE

Most bugs lay eggs, and their young develop through a series of stages. Certain insects such as butterflies, moths, flies, wasps, bees and beetles undergo a process such as the one shown below. In this process, the bug takes various different forms between the egg stage and the adult stage.

THE TAILED JAY BUTTERFLY – FROM EGG TO ADULT

An adult female tailed jay lays an egg on a leaf. The egg usually takes between three and four days to hatch.

A caterpillar (known as a **LARVA**) hatches from the egg. It is very small when it first emerges, but it has a big appetite and as it eats, it grows much larger.

Bugs such as cockroaches and grasshoppers undergo a simpler process in which a smaller version of the adult emerges from the egg. This is known as a **NYMPH**. The nymph grows, shedding its outer skeleton in stages before finally reaching its adult size.

A small number of bugs (such as **APHIDS**) give birth to live young, but this is not very common.

The caterpillar then becomes a **PUPA**. This process is known as **METAMORPHOSIS**. The pupa is fixed to a leaf and remains there whilst the caterpillar's body breaks down into goo and reforms into a butterfly.

The fully-formed butterfly emerges from the pupa after about two weeks, and then flies away. The insect's final adult form is known as the **IMAGO**.

THE ANATOMY OF BUGS

Bugs come in all shapes, sizes, colours and patterns.
Despite that, all bugs have the same basic body structure.

The **head capsule** contains the brain. The hard exterior
of the head is home to the bug's eyes, its **ANTENNAE** and
mouthparts.

The **thorax** contains the first section of the bug's gut and
circulatory system. The wings (if present) and legs are
attached to the thorax.

The **abdomen** contains the remainder of the guts, the
heart, the reproductive organs and, if the insect has one,
its sting!

EXTERNAL ANATOMY

Despite their vastly differing shapes, most bugs have a relatively similar anatomy. Here we look at the external features of the **giant burrowing cockroach** – *Macropanesthia rhinoceros.*

As we already know, all bugs have a **head** (1), **thorax** (2) and an **abdomen** (3).

Bugs also all have sensory **antennae** (4) attached to their heads.

The bug's thorax is divided into three different areas, the front **prothorax** (5), central **mesothorax** (6), and rear **metathorax** (7).

Similarly, the bug's legs are described according to their position, with the **foreleg** (8) in front of the **middle leg** (9) and the **hind leg** (10) at the rear.

The **CERCI** (11) at the bug's rear are sometimes sensory organs or can also function as pinching weapons. In many bugs they no longer have any useful function and are then known as **VESTIGIAL STRUCTURES**.

On the underside of the head are the **mouthparts** (12).

The section of the leg that attaches to the bug's thorax is called the **coxa** (13). The next section is called the **trochanter** (14).

The **femur** (15) and **tibia** (16) usually form the longest section of the bug's leg.

At the end of each leg is the **tarsus** (17), which is usually formed of five separate segments. At the end of the tarsus is a pair of **claws** (18). Some insects also have pads on the base of the tarsus, known as **arolia**.

Bugs which do a lot of digging often have larger, more heavily muscled forelegs. Jumping bugs typically have much longer hind legs that help them to leap high into the air.

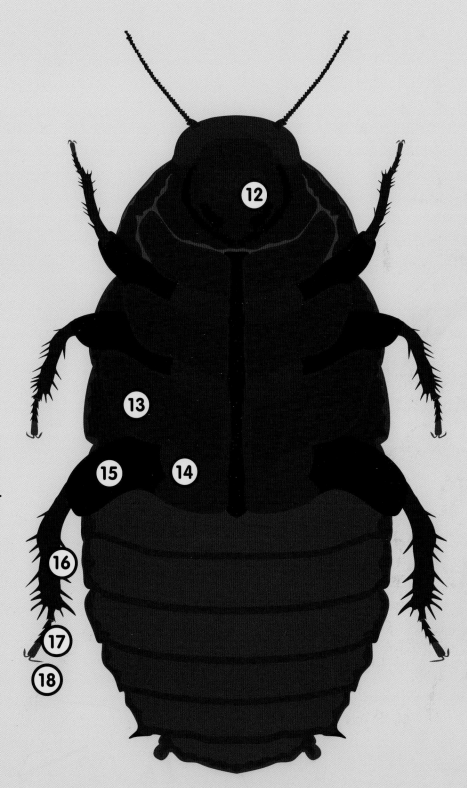

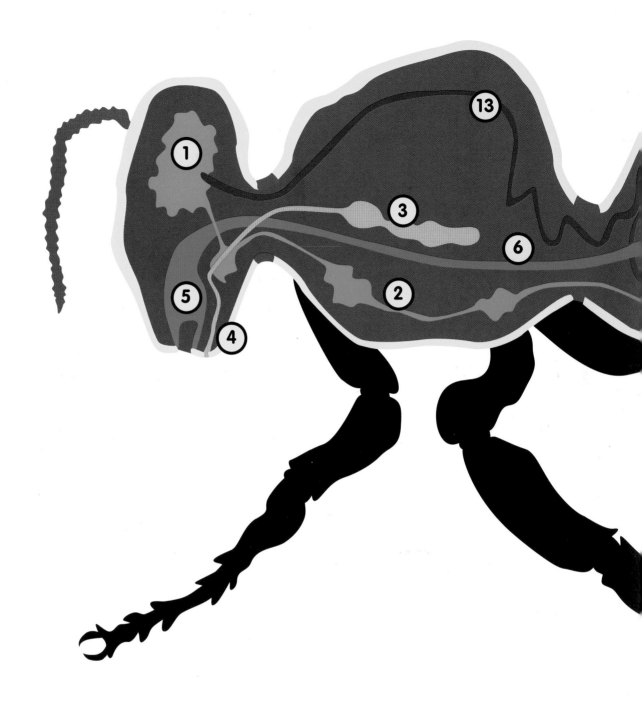

INTERNAL ANATOMY

Most bugs also share similar internal anatomy. Here we see the internal structure of the **western honey bee** – *Apis mellifera*.

The bee's **brain** (1) is in its head. It connects to the rest of the nervous system via the **nerve cord** (2) which runs along the bee's belly.

The bee produces saliva in the **salivary gland** (3), which is connected to the **salivary duct** (4) near its **mouth** (5). The saliva helps with digestion and also when the bee is feeding larvae in the nest. Food that the bee eats passes along a tube called the **oesophagus** (6) into the **crop** (7) where it is stored. When the bee returns to the nest, it can regurgitate nectar from the crop to

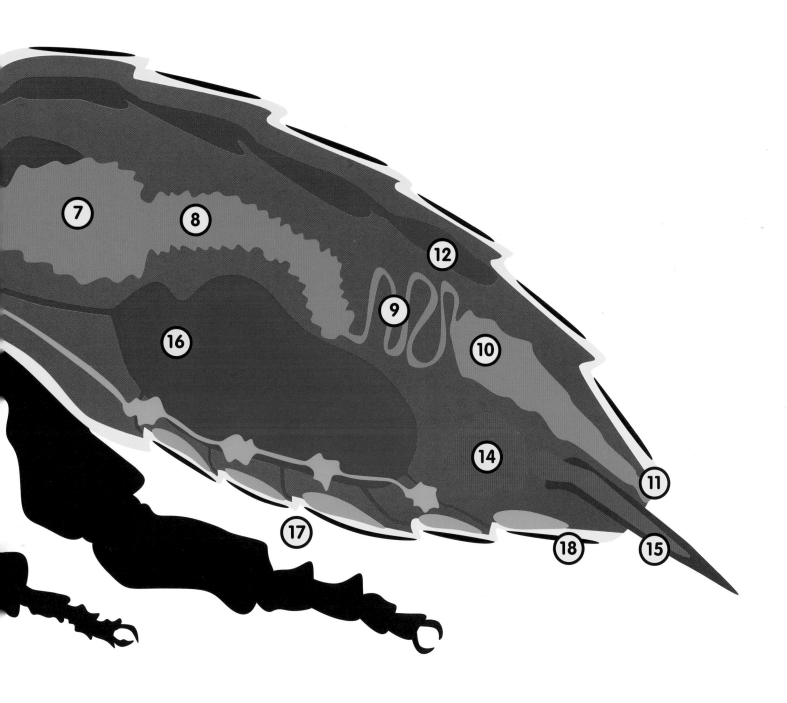

be stored in the nest. The remaining food (mostly pollen) passes into the **stomach** (8) where it is digested. Nutrients and water are absorbed in the **intestine** (9), and then waste is held in the **rectum** (10) before being excreted out of the **anus** (11).

The bee's **heart** (12) pumps its **HAEMOLYMPH** forwards, towards the brain via a tube called the **aorta** (13). The bee's **poison sac** (14) stores the toxic chemicals for its **sting** (15).

The bee breathes with an **air sac** (16) that pumps in air through holes in the abdomen called **spiracles** (17). The bee produces wax for nest building in **wax glands** (18) on its lower abdomen.

BUG EYES

Most bugs have **COMPOUND EYES**, which are made up of hundreds of separate units called **OMMATIDIA** grouped in a pattern like a mosaic. These are usually found on either side of the bug's head (such as the **bluebottle fly** – *Calliphora vomitoria* – below) but can also meet in the middle of the head.

Compound eyes allow a very wide field of vision. This helps bugs to spot any **PREDATORS** lurking to the side or even behind them. They are also good for judging distances – useful to help hunting insects to pounce on their prey.

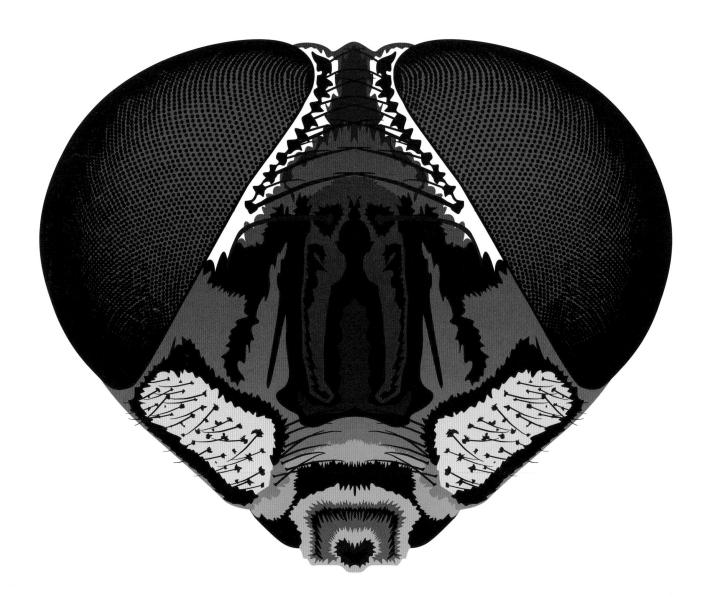

Certain bugs have both large compound eyes and simple eyes, known as **OCELLI**. These are often found towards the back or top of the head (such as the red ocelli on the head of the **African mantis** – *Sphodromantis lineola* – below). Bugs do not use ocelli to see, but to detect small changes in light levels. This helps them to find their way around by positioning themselves compared to the sun.

Certain insects (usually those that live in caves or underground) have just ocelli, or sometimes no eyes at all. They instead use other senses to navigate their world.

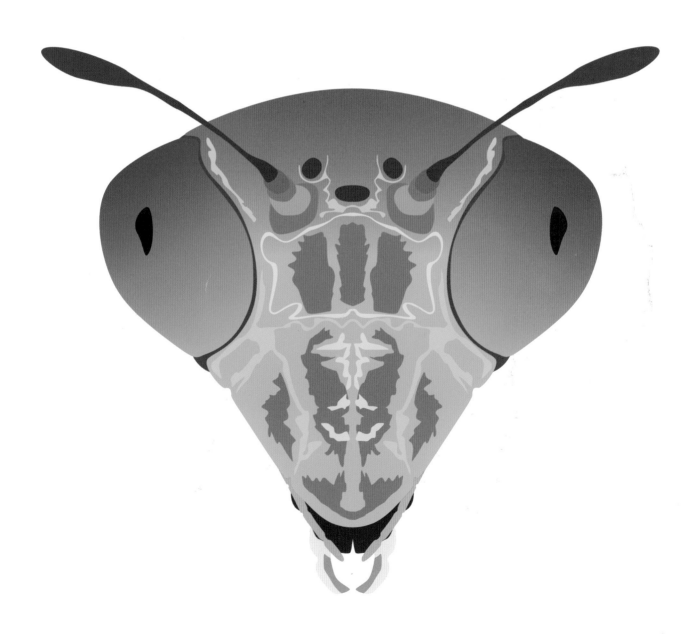

OTHER BUG SENSES

As well as using their eyes, bugs have other ways of sensing the world around them. The main way they do this is through the use of their antennae. All adult bugs have antennae, but their shape, size and sensitivity varies across species.

The main function of the antennae is to detect smells. Each antenna has sensors called **OLFACTORY RECEPTORS** that detect the presence of the chemicals that produce smells. It then transmits this information to the bug's brain. The chemical smells might be caused by food, or by the presence of other bugs.

If smell is very important to the bug, the antennae tend to be more complex, with feathery fronds. These increase the area of the antennae, to boost sensitivity.

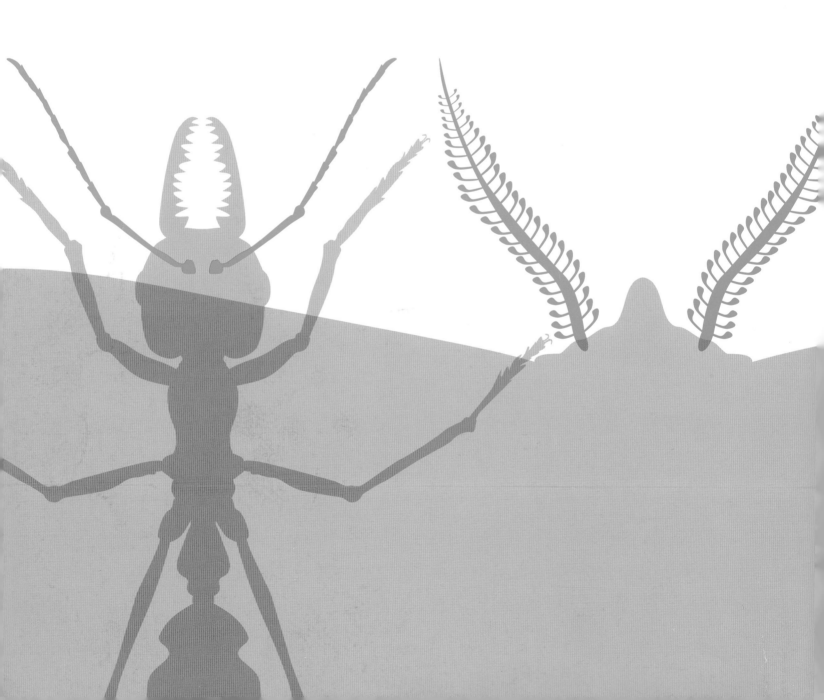

Bugs also use their antennae as feelers. Touch sensors in the antennae allow the bug to sense the presence of objects in front of them. These sensors can also detect wind movement and vibrations.

Some bugs also have other sense organs on different parts of their bodies. Crickets have hearing sensors called **TYMPANEL ORGANS** on their hind legs, and grasshoppers have similar sensors on the sides of their abdomen.

Some insects, like flies, have taste-detecting sensors in their feet, allowing them to identify sweet foods just by landing on them!

BUG DEFENCES

Because of their small size, many bugs are vulnerable to being eaten by predators, including other bugs. For that reason, they have evolved a number of defensive strategies to protect themselves.

POISON and BRIGHT COLOURS

Because bugs in the larval stage can be vulnerable to attack, many have evolved effective defences. The **cinnabar moth caterpillar** – *Tyria jacobaeae* – below, eats poisonous ragwort leaves, and this toxin builds up in the caterpillar's body. If a predator tries to eat the caterpillar, it will taste disgusting, and may even kill them. Because the species has evolved a distinctive bright yellow striped pattern, predators have learned to avoid eating them.

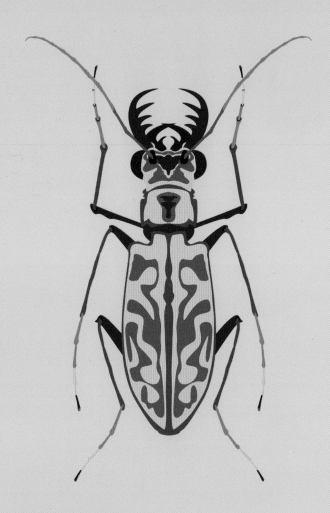

WEAPONRY

Bugs often have spines, stings and large mouthparts that they can use to defend themselves. Certain beetles can respond to an attack aggressively, and species such as the **mudflat tiger beetle** – *Cicindela trifasciata sigmoidea* – above, will give a painful bite. Other bugs, such as the **Asian giant hornet** – *Vespa mandarinia* – have powerful stings which can seriously hurt or kill anything that tries to eat them.

DISGUISE

Certain bugs, particularly butterflies and moths, such as the **io moth** – *Automeris io* – above, have patterns that resemble a large pair of eyes. These trick potential predators, such as small birds, into thinking that the bug is actually a dangerous, larger bird.

BUG SPRAY

Other bugs have evolved a particularly off-putting defensive mechanism – they are able to spray or squirt foul liquids at any would-be predators. For example, the **green shield bug** – *Palomena prasina* – left, can produce toxic chemicals in a gland on its abdomen. When it feels threatened, it can eject this chemical as a liquid, which deters most predators.

WHAT DO BUGS EAT?

Bugs eat an enormously varied range of foods, and have developed all sorts of clever strategies for getting it. They have also evolved some amazingly complex mouthparts to help them suck it up or gobble it down. Some are even able to grow their own food.

Many insects are **CARNIVOROUS** predators, including mantids, dragonflies, some true bugs and some beetles. Tiger beetles are, for their size, one of the most formidable predators on Earth. They can move very fast, and catch other insects and spiders with their powerful, sharp mouthparts.

Dragonflies are brilliant aerial predators, and can catch and eat their prey during flight, without putting a foot on the ground.

Most butterflies and moths have developed specialist mouthparts adapted to drinking liquid food, such as plant nectar, tree sap and rotting fruit juices.

Others are more adaptable, such as bees, which can lap up liquid nectar and also deal with solid food too, such as pollen.

Some ants and termites bring plant material into their nests, onto which they are able to grow fungi. They then use the fungi as a source of food – ingenious!

The diet of many insect species even differs between the males and females. For example, the females of many flies such as mosquitoes, horseflies and biting midges drink blood, but the males feed on nectar. This is because the females need extra proteins from a blood meal to produce eggs. This strategy is known as **ANAUTOGENY**.

Most bugs ensure that their offspring can eat when they hatch by laying eggs on the larvae's preferred food. For example, **burying beetles** get their name because they actively search for small dead rodents or birds. They then dig a hole and bury the dead creature, and the female lays her eggs on it. When the larvae hatch, their parents feed them from the rotting carcass.

The **differential grasshopper** – *Melanoplus differentialis* – opposite, has a voracious appetite and particularly likes the young shoots of farmed crops such as corn, soy and fruit trees. Swarms of these grasshoppers can destroy huge volumes of crops, which is a major problem for farmers in the southern United States and Mexico.

HOW DO BUGS EAT?

Butterflies and moths use a long tube called a **PROBOSCIS** to suck nectar from flowers. The eating method that these bugs use is called **SIPHONING**. The bug's proboscis is flexible and it can curl up into a tight roll when not being used for feeding. They can be very long, in the case of the **Morgan's sphinx moth** – *Xanthopan morgani* – over 300mm in length.

Bees have a tongue-like structure called a **LABIUM.** They use this to dip into nectar or honey, which is picked up on tiny hairs and then drawn into the mouth with a pumping action. Bees also have **MANDIBLES**, but these are mainly used for shaping nest materials.

Some bugs, such as beetles, mantids and ants, have two large appendages called chewing mandibles, which they use to bite, tear and chew their food. Smaller structures underneath the mandibles, called **MAXILLARY PALPS**, transfer food into the mouth. Bugs that eat in this way are known as mandibulates.

True bugs, fleas, sucking lice and biting flies (such as mosquitoes) also use a proboscis for feeding. However, the proboscises used by these bugs are rigid and are used for piercing tissue and then drawing liquids out of both animals and plants. The eating technique that these bugs use is called pierce-sucking.

HOW DO BUGS GET AROUND?

Bugs have evolved a number of methods for moving around, which is one of the reasons they have become so successful at adapting to different habitats and climates.

FLYING

Of all the flying insects, butterflies and moths possess the largest and most beautiful wings. Their wings are made of very thin layers of **CHITIN,** covered with tiny scales. It is these scales that are responsible for pattern and colour, as observed on the **sapho longwing** – *Heliconius sapho* – below.

At rest, the butterfly can move each of its four wings separately, but when it takes off, the fore and hindwings on each side lock together and the butterfly moves them as one. As the butterfly flaps its wings, it also moves them in a twisting figure-of-eight motion, and this lifts the butterfly into the air and moves it forward. Butterflies beat their wings between 5 and 12 times every second.

Bugs such as flies, bees, beetles and wasps, including the **thread-waisted potter wasp** – *Phimenes flavopictus* – above, have very fine transparent or translucent wings. These are also made of chitin, but there are no scales present. They can vary in colour and pattern depending on the thickness of the chitin and any patterns on the surface of the wings.

These bugs are able to beat their wings at very high speeds. Most fly wings beat around 100 times a second, and wasp wings beat up to 400 times per second. The fastest recorded wing beaters are **biting midges** – *Forcipomyia squamipennis* – which can exceed 1000 beats per second.

The tiniest flying insects use a method known as "clap and fling" rather than conventional aerodynamics. This involves them "clapping" their wings above them, and then "flinging" them down. This creates lift, but damages the insect's wings over time.

WALKING

As we have already discovered, all bugs have six legs, and all bugs use them to walk. The most efficient walking method used involves keeping three legs on the ground and moving the other three forwards. This is known as a tripedal gait.

We can observe this walking style in the movement of the **plagionotus beetle** – *Plagionotus astecus* – on the right.

1 – In the first picture we see the beetle standing still. In this position the beetle is standing on all 6 legs.

2 – In the second picture the beetle lifts three legs (coloured red) and moves them forwards. As it does this, its body swings to one side. By remaining standing on two legs on one side and one on the other, it remains stable.

3 – In the third picture the beetle lifts up the other three legs (coloured blue), and moves them forwards. As it does this, its body swings the other way.

2 and 3 continue in alternating fashion while the beetle is in motion.

4 – The beetle stops, standing on all six legs.

Bugs are very adaptable, and can use other gaits. For example, if they lose a leg they are able to use a modified version of the tripedal gait, moving two legs on one side rather than three.

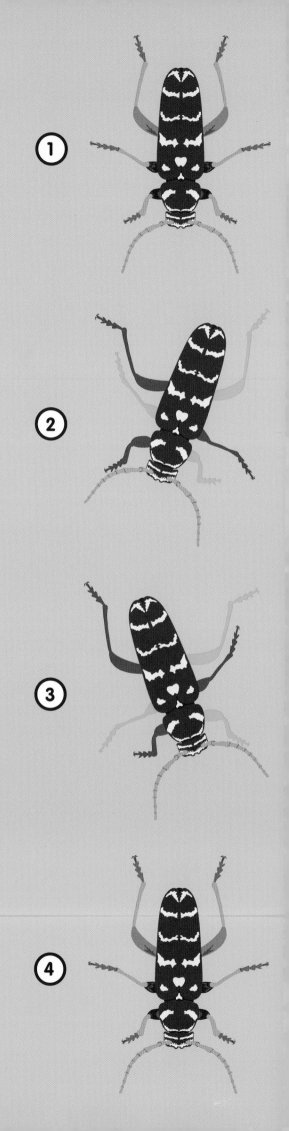

SWIMMING

Some bugs, such as the **greater water boatman** – *Notonecta glauca* – are able to swim very effectively. Often called **backswimmers** because they swim upside down, using their backs like a little boat, their hind legs are long and have evolved a series of hairy fronds along their edges. They use these long legs like paddles to propel themselves across the surfaces of lakes, ponds, and marshes. They catch and eat tadpoles, small fish and other insects.

Other bugs can propel themselves through the water by thrashing their bodies like fish (insect larvae and mayfly **NYMPHS**), and others can even get around by squirting water out of their bottoms (dragonfly nymphs)!

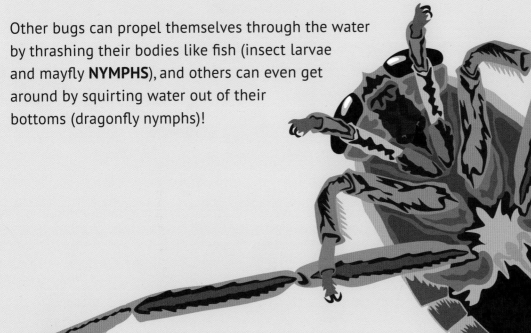
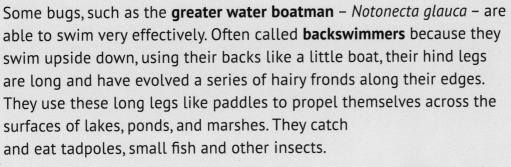

WHERE DO BUGS LIVE?

The majority of bugs live on land, and most of them spend a lot of their time on their own. They usually live and sleep close to their main source of food, and only live with other bugs when it's time to reproduce. As such, they are known as solitary insects.

A number of bug species live in groups, called **COLONIES**. These can range from nests of a few individuals to many thousands.

Certain bugs, like ants, some bees and termites, live in large colonies in which they have specific jobs. Groups of bugs which live in such groups are known as **EUSOCIAL**. Eusocial bugs cooperate with one another to take care of the young, produced by a single or a few females in the group.

Paper wasps – *Polistes dominula* – are a type of social wasp that constructs open-celled nests such as the one above. They collect wood which they chew to form a papery pulp to construct their nests. Their saliva contains a sticky substance that makes the pulp very strong and also remarkably waterproof. Paper wasp colonies usually contain up to 200 individual wasps.

INSIDE A TERMITE MOUND

Termite mounds like the one below are home to colonies that can contain up to a million individual termites. The termites live in **galleries (1)** below ground level, and the mound has a sophisticated ventilation system so they don't get too hot, including a **ventilation chimney (2)**, which draws cooler air from the lowest point in the mound – the **cellar (3)**.

They venture out at night (when it's cooler) through their **escape tunnels (4)**, and collect food which can include plant material, wood and animal dung. They bring their goodies back to the nest where some of it is eaten. Any foraged wood or dense plant material is chewed up and then goes into their **fungus combs (5)** – areas of the nest where they grow fungus on the wood pulp. This fungus produces sugars that the termites use as a food source within the nest.

Like the paper wasps, the termites mix their nest-building materials in their mouths. In the termites' case, the mixture is mainly clay soil and their own waste material, which they mix with their saliva. They lay this down one blob at a time. When dry it is very tough and long-lasting. Some termite mounds have reached over twelve metres in height.

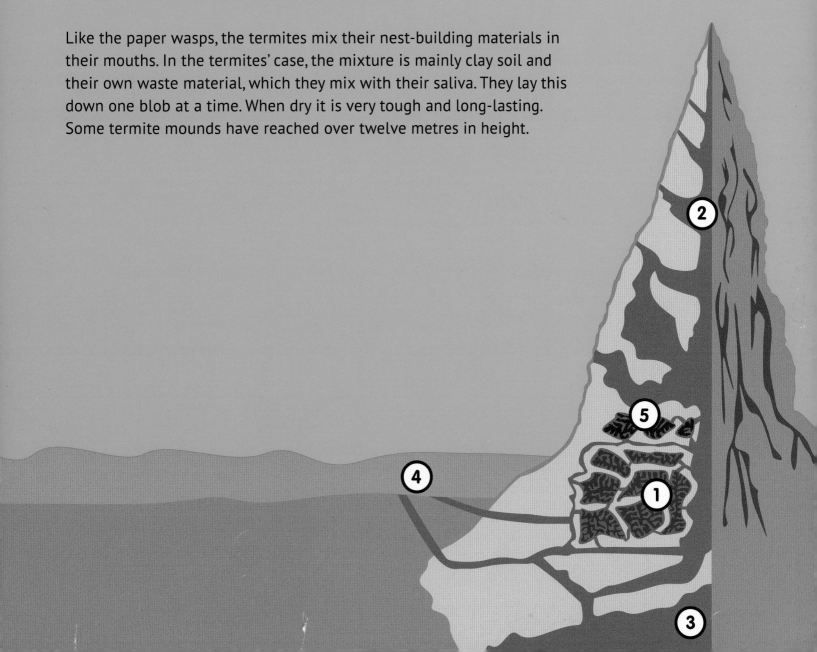

BEETLES

Beetles are a group of insects that make up the order *coleoptera*. They are the most diverse of all animal orders, and are found in nearly every habitat apart from the oceans and the polar regions. There are over 400,000 known species of beetle.

Most beetles eat plant matter, but certain species such as **scarab beetles** eat dung, and a number are predatory, such as the highly aggressive **tiger beetles.**

Beetles have two pairs of wings, but the top pair has evolved to form a hard, protective sheath which covers the delicate second pair underneath.

Blue-spotted tiger beetle
Cicindela aurulenta
Length: 20mm

Found in Asia, particularly China, Indonesia, Malaysia and Thailand

Like other tiger beetles, this species is a quick-moving predator. It feeds on smaller insects and other small animals.

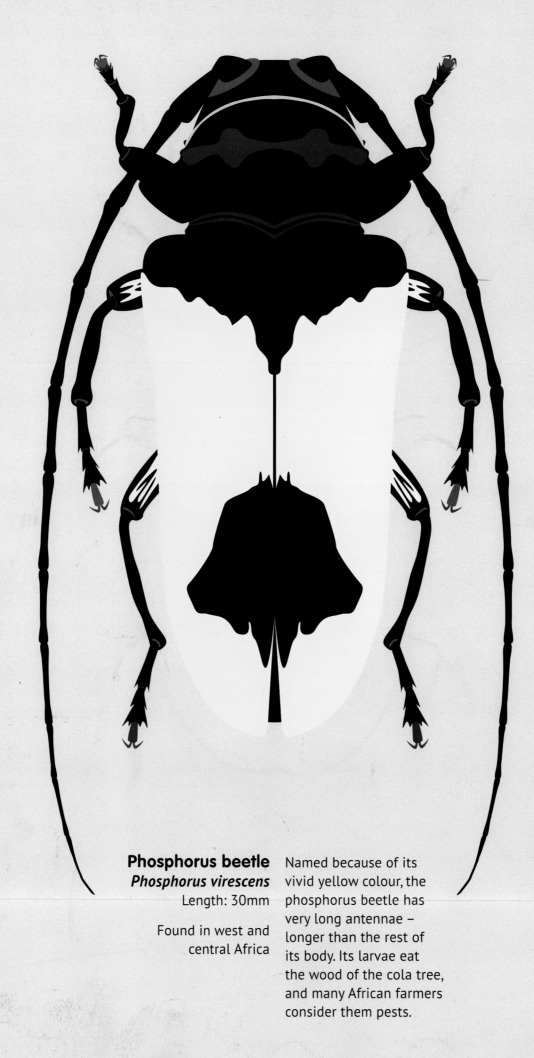

Phosphorus beetle
Phosphorus virescens
Length: 30mm

Found in west and
central Africa

Named because of its
vivid yellow colour, the
phosphorus beetle has
very long antennae –
longer than the rest of
its body. Its larvae eat
the wood of the cola tree,
and many African farmers
consider them pests.

Cardinal beetle
Pyrochroa serraticornis
Length: 15mm

Found across
western Europe

Cardinal beetles are
predatory, and feed on
smaller insects. Their
carnivorous larvae are
often found amongst
loose, rotting tree bark.

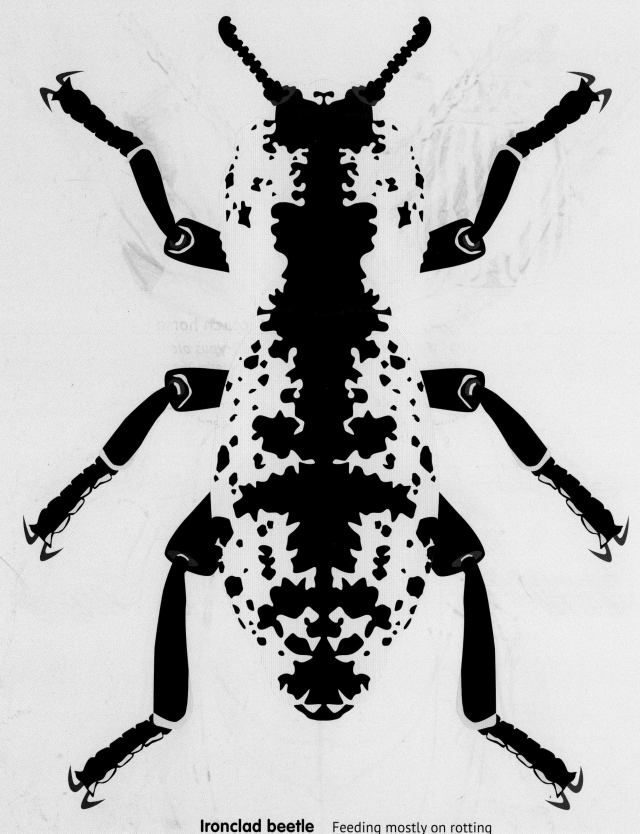

Ironclad beetle

Zopherus nodulosus

Length: 25mm

Found in the southwestern US, and central and northern South America

Feeding mostly on rotting wood and plant material, ironclad beetles get their name because their exoskeleton is one of the hardest of all insects. They are also known as the death feigning beetle, because they often play dead when attacked.

Colorado potato beetle
Leptinotarsa decemlineata
Length: 10mm

Found across the USA and Mexico

This species gets its name because it is a major agricultural pest. It can cause great damage to potato crops, and also tomato and aubergine plants.

Devil's coach horse
Ocypus olens
Length: 25mm

Found across Europe, North Africa, and North America

An aggressive nocturnal predator, the devil's coach horse eats slugs, spiders and worms. When threatened it raises its tail like a scorpion and defends itself with its large mandibles.

Violin beetle
Mormolyce phyllodes
Length: 90mm

Found in the rainforests of southeast Asia

Named because its shape resembles a violin, this beetle has a very flat body which allows it to live in narrow gaps under bark, inside cracks in the soil and in between layers of bracket fungi. If attacked, it can secrete a powerful acid which can paralyse the predator while the beetle escapes.

Christmas beetle
Anoplognathus pallidicollis
Length: 20mm

Found in Australia

Known as the Christmas beetle because it is commonly seen in the Australian summer month of December, this beetle mainly feeds on eucalyptus foliage.

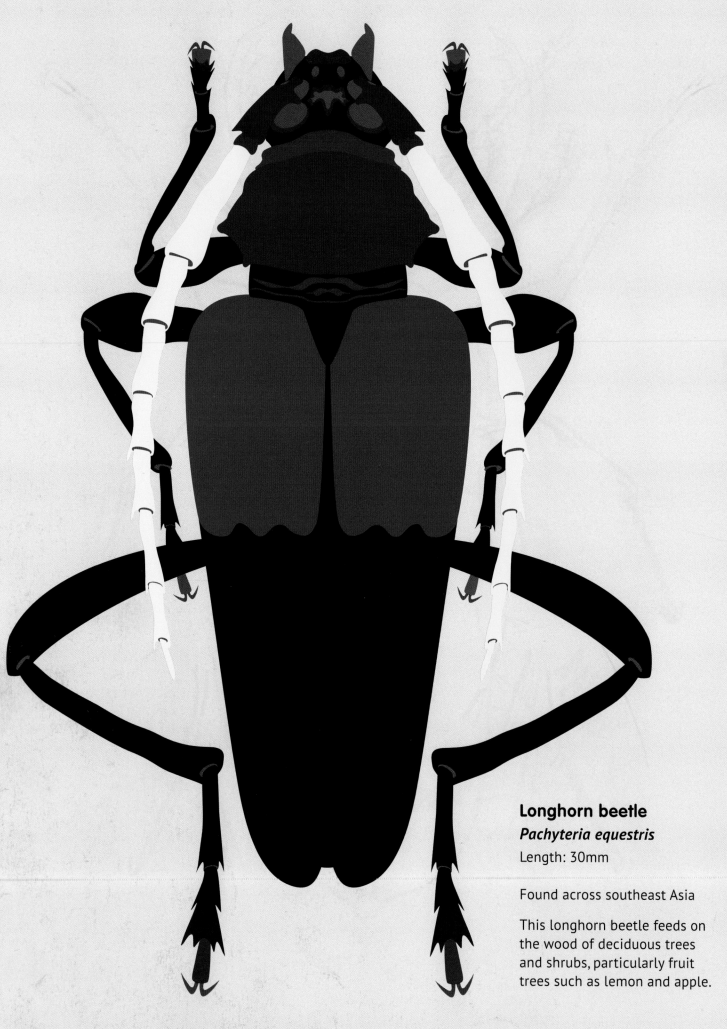

Longhorn beetle
Pachyteria equestris
Length: 30mm

Found across southeast Asia

This longhorn beetle feeds on
the wood of deciduous trees
and shrubs, particularly fruit
trees such as lemon and apple.

Orange ladybird
Halyzia sedecimguttata
Length: 6mm

Found across Europe
and North Africa

Common in woodland
environments, the
orange ladybird feeds on
mildew fungus and small
aphids.

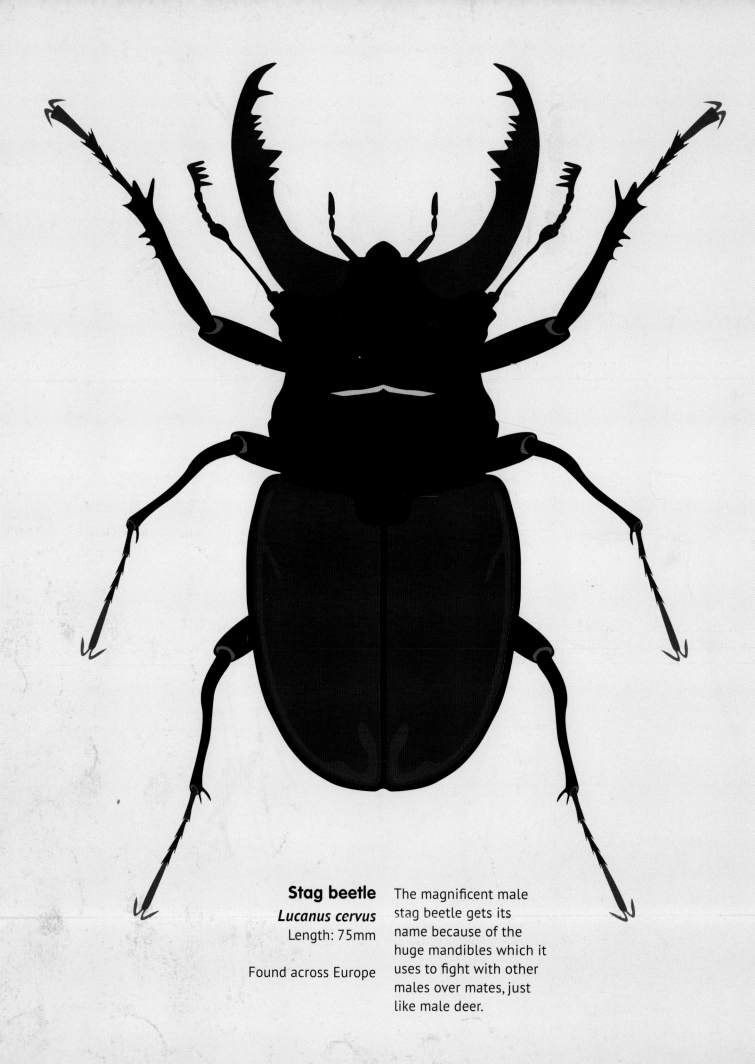

Stag beetle

Lucanus cervus
Length: 75mm

Found across Europe

The magnificent male stag beetle gets its name because of the huge mandibles which it uses to fight with other males over mates, just like male deer.

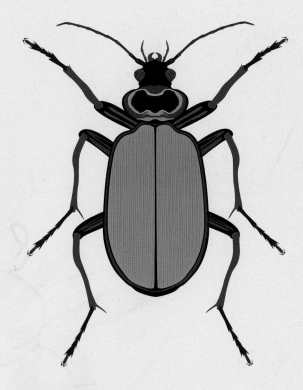

Giraffe weevil
Trachelophorus giraffa
Length: 80mm

Found on the African island of Madagascar

The male giraffe weevil gets its name from its long neck which, like the stag beetle, is used during fighting for a mate.

Caterpillar hunter
Calosoma scrutator
Length: 30mm

Found across North America

As its name suggests, this ground-living beetle predates on caterpillars. It can release a substance when attacked which smells like rotting milk!

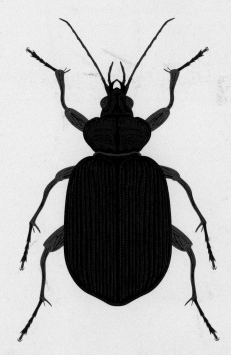

Green tiger beetle
Cicindela campestris
Length: 15mm

Found across Europe

Another predatory species, the larvae of the green tiger beetle dig holes in the ground to catch smaller insects such as ants.

Green carab beetle
Calosoma schayeri
Length: 27mm

Found across Australia

This beetle is attracted to bright lights and so is often seen in city centres!

BEES, WASPS AND ANTS

Bees, wasps and ants make up the insect order *hymenoptera*.
There are over 280,000 known species in the order.

The order contains a number of species with highly evolved social systems,
such as honey bees and ants.

Most hymenopterans have thin, membranous wings. Some of them, such as ants,
only have their wings for a portion of their adult life before they shed them.

Many of them also have a powerful sting at the tip of their abdomen, which they
use as defence against predators. The sting is unique to *hymenoptera*.

Tarantula hawk
Pepsis mildei
Length: 25 - 50mm

Found across the
southern USA through
Central America to
northern South America

This species gets its
name because it hunts
and feeds on tarantula
spiders. It has an
extremely powerful and
painful sting, second
only to that of the bullet
ant.

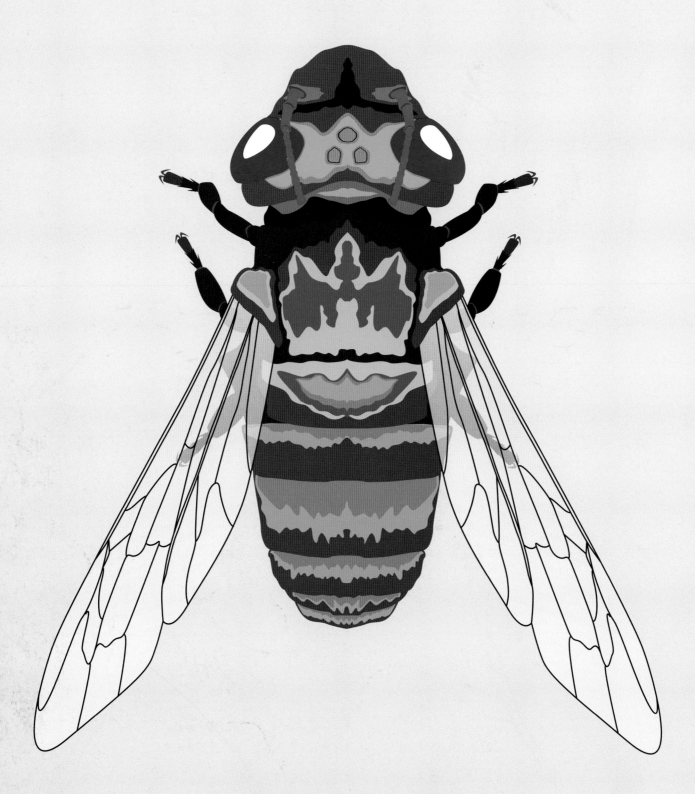

Orchid bee
Euglossa imperialis
Length: 19mm

Found across Central
and South America

The orchid bee gets
its name because it
feeds on orchid nectar
and as such is of great
importance in the
pollination of orchids.

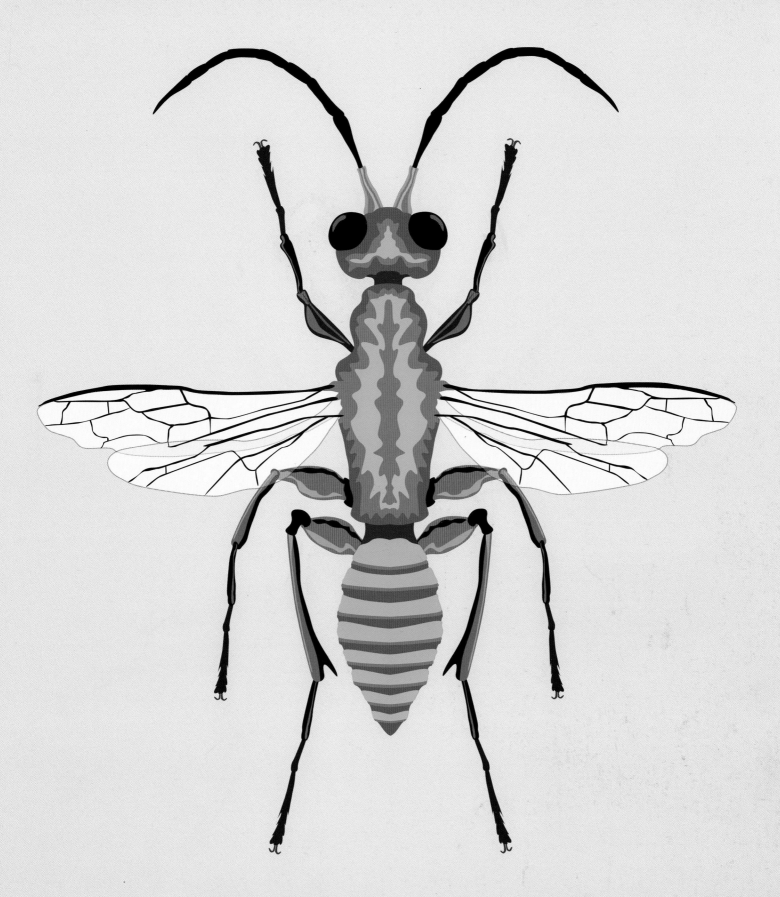

Emerald cockroach wasp
Ampulex compressa
Length: 20mm

Found in southeast Asia
and tropical Africa

Also known as the jewel wasp,
the female of this solitary
wasp species paralyses a
cockroach with its toxic sting
before laying an egg inside it.
When the larva emerges it
feeds on the dying cockroach.

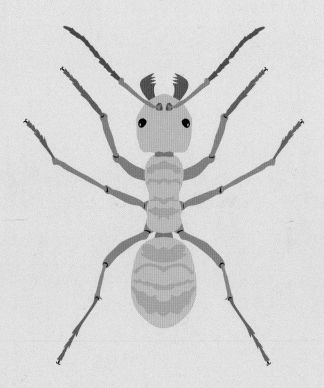

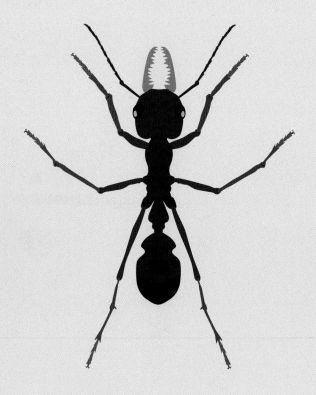

Yellow meadow ant
Lasius flavus
Length: 20mm

Found worldwide

This ant species lives in grassland areas, and feeds on honeydew secreted by aphids living in the soil around the roots of the grass.

Red bull ant
Myrmecia gulosa
Length: 25mm

Found across Australia

These ants are aggressive predators able to kill and feed on larger insects such as bees.

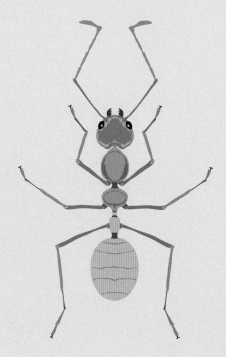

Green-headed ant
Rhytidoponera metallica
Length: 6mm

Found across Australia

Green-headed ants have a widely-varied diet, feeding on everything from beetles and termites to plant material, particularly plant seeds.

Weaver ant
Oecophylla smaragdina
Length: 6mm

Found across Asia and Australia

Weaver ants get their name because they create nests in the tree canopy by weaving leaves together with silk made by their larvae.

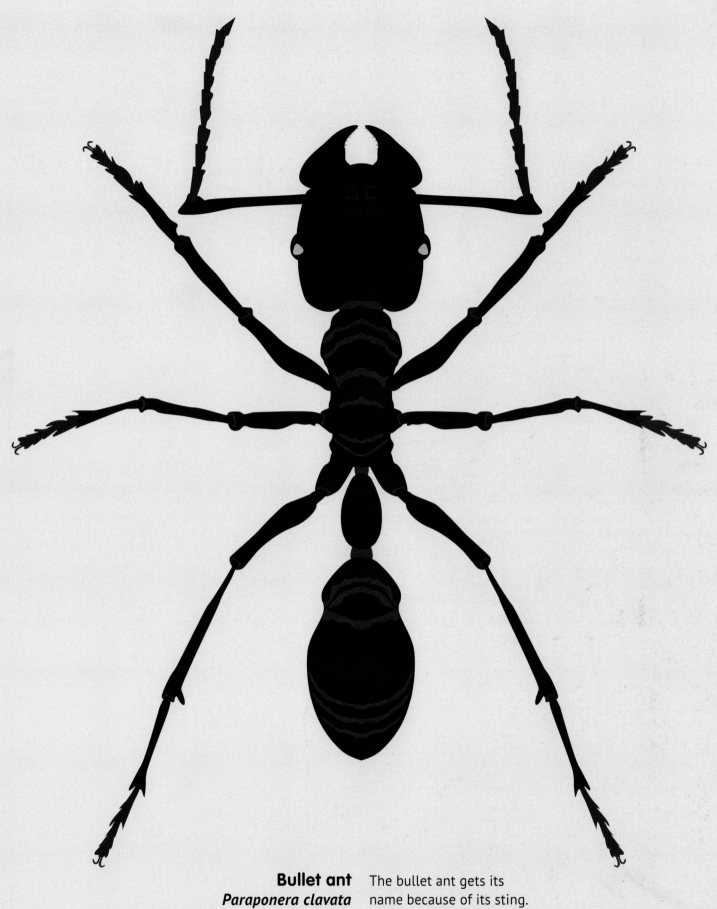

Bullet ant
Paraponera clavata
Length: 25mm

Found across Central
America and northern
South America

The bullet ant gets its
name because of its sting.
It is reputed to be the
most painful of any insect
species. The sting toxin is
extremely powerful and can
cause paralysis in humans.

BUTTERFLIES AND MOTHS

Butterflies and moths make up the insect order *lepidoptera*. There are over 200,000 known species in the order.

Both butterflies and moths have evolved a huge variety in wing pattern and colouration. Some use earthy colours as camouflage, while some have developed patterns that look like eyes, to scare potential predators. Others have very bright, striking colours that help them attract a mate, or warn predators that they are poisonous.

Most butterflies and moths feed on nectar or sap from plants, but some live purely on fat reserves they stored up during their larval stage.

White dragontail
Lamproptera curius
Wingspan: 50mm

Found in southeast Asia, particularly India, southern China, Indonesia, Malaysia and Thailand

The white dragontail is a species of swallowtail butterfly which is always found near streams or rivers, and is a rapid flyer.

Blue morpho
Morpho helenor
Wingspan: 115mm

Found across Central
America and northern
South America

The iridescent
blue morpho typically
feeds on the juices
of rotting fruit.

Dido longwing
Philaethria dido
Wingspan: 110mm

Found across Central
America and northern
South America

The dido longwing usually
lives high in the Amazonian
forest canopy, but flies
down occasionally to drink
from mineral-rich streams.

Peacock butterfly
Aglais io
Wingspan: 50mm

Found across Europe and Asia

The peacock butterfly uses the distinctive eye-like markings on its wings to scare off small birds, and sounds to scare off rodents.

Viceroy
Limenitis archippus
Wingspan: 65mm

Found across North America and Mexico

Viceroy caterpillars feed on willow wood, which builds up concentrations of salicylic acid, making them foul-tasting to potential predators.

Garden tiger moth
Arctia caja
Wingspan: 60mm

Found across Europe,
central Asia and
North America

The brightly-patterned
wings of the garden tiger
moth act to scare off
potential predators,
warning them that
the moth contains
poisonous toxins.

Elephant hawk moth
Deilephila elpenor
Wingspan: 60mm

Found across
Europe and Asia

This moth has extremely
good vision in low light,
which enables it to find
flowers at night to feed on
nectar.

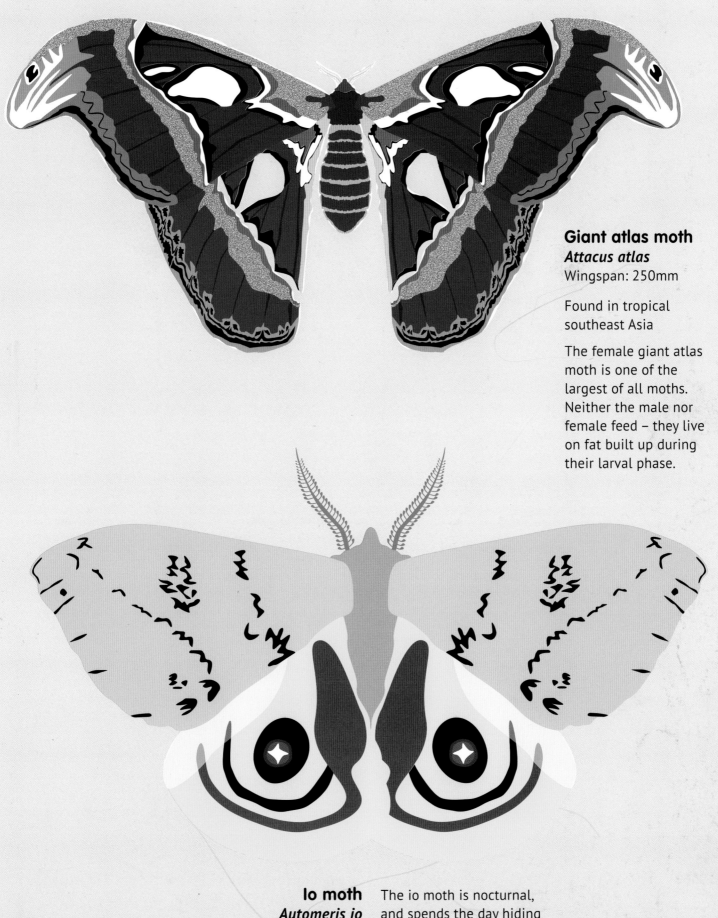

Giant atlas moth
Attacus atlas
Wingspan: 250mm

Found in tropical southeast Asia

The female giant atlas moth is one of the largest of all moths. Neither the male nor female feed – they live on fat built up during their larval phase.

Io moth
Automeris io
Wingspan: 70mm

Found across North America

The io moth is nocturnal, and spends the day hiding in yellowing leaves. It uses the eye-like pattern on its wings as a defence against potential predators.

**Madagascan
sunset moth**
Chrysiridia rhipheus
Wingspan: 85mm

Found on the African
island of Madagascar

This magnificent
moth has iridescent
colourations on its
wings, and feeds on
nectar from mostly
white-flowered plants,
such as almond, tea,
and loquat.

Sylphina angel
Chorinea sylphina
Wingspan: 35mm

Found in Ecuador,
Bolivia and Peru

This butterfly lives in the
cloud forests of South
America and feeds on
the nectar of flowering
forest plants.

Bhutan glory
Bhutanitis lidderdalii
Wingspan: 110mm

Found across India and
southern Asia

This swallowtail butterfly
lives at altitudes of nearly
3,000 metres in the
mountains of India and
Bhutan.

Tailed jay
Graphium Agamemnon
Wingspan: 95mm

Found across India and southern Asia

The tailed jay is another swallowtail
butterfly that is particularly energetic
– it often continues to flap its wings
even when it has landed on a plant to
feed.

Rajah Brooke's birdwing
Trogonoptera brookiana
Wingspan: 170mm

Found across southern Asia

The beautiful Rajah Brooke's birdwing is endangered as its natural habitat is being destroyed to create farmland and urban areas.

Painted lady
Vanessa cardui
Wingspan: 80mm

Found worldwide

Female painted lady butterflies lay many eggs for their size, and their species migrates from Africa to the Arctic Circle and back, over successive generations.

Citrus swallowtail
Papilio demodocus

Wingspan: 110mm

Found across
sub-Saharan Africa and
the Arabian Peninsula

This species gets its name because the female adult lays her eggs on the leaves of citrus trees, which are then eaten by the hatching larvae. It is also known as the Christmas butterfly, because it is most frequently spotted during the month of December.

TRUE BUGS

True bugs are a group of insects that form the order *hemiptera*. It is a diverse group, with a great variety of scale, shape and adaptation on display.

All true bugs have pierce-sucking mouthparts, allowing them to extract sap from plants or, in some cases, blood from larger animals. Some hemipterans are predatory and feed on other insects and creatures.

Whilst most are harmless to humans, certain species cause great problems for farmers, as they can devastate crops and spread fungal plant diseases. Other species are beneficial for pest control, by eating pest hemipterans like aphids.

Green shield bug
Palomena prasina
Length: 15mm

Found across Europe

This species is also known as the green stink bug because, like many other shield bugs, it can excrete a very smelly liquid to frighten off potential predators. It is very common, and easy to spot in the summer months.

Giant mesquite bug
Thasus neocalifornicus
Length: 35mm

Found in the southwestern
US and Mexico

This colourful bug gets
its name because it feeds
on the young leaves, sap
and seed pods of the
mesquite tree.

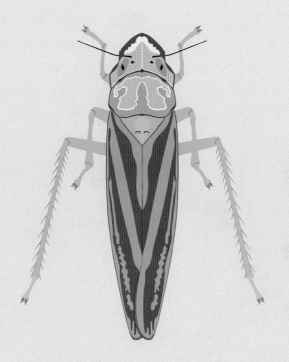

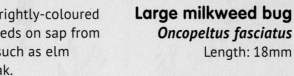

Candy-striped leafhopper
Graphocephala coccinea
Length: 8mm

Found in North and Central America

This brightly-coloured bug feeds on sap from trees such as elm and oak.

Large milkweed bug
Oncopeltus fasciatus
Length: 18mm

Found across North and Central America

The milkweed bug's bright patterns act to warn off potential predators, as the bug contains toxic chemicals.

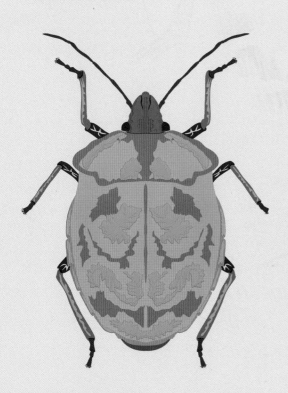

Cotton harlequin bug
Tectocoris diophthalmus
Length: 20mm

Found in Australia and the Pacific Islands

This bug lives in rainforests and coastal regions, and feeds on nectar from hibiscus flowers.

Jewel bug
Pachycoris torridus
Length: 15mm

Found in northern South America

Jewel bugs often cluster together in groups for defence from predators.

DRAGONFLIES AND DAMSELFLIES

Dragonflies and damselflies make up the order *odonata*. This order contains around 6,000 species.

The members of the order are characterised by their features for hunting in flight. They are all efficient hunters, with spiny legs for catching prey and excellent eyesight thanks to their large compound eyes.

They also have two pairs of long wings, and their flying abilities are impressive. Certain dragonfly species can reach speeds of over 90 kilometres per hour – they can even fly backwards and upside-down!

Emperor dragonfly
Anax imperator
Wingspan: 120 mm

Found across Europe, North Africa and Asia

This species is fairly common in the UK, where it is typically spotted hovering over ponds, streams and marshy ground.

Its favoured prey includes small butterflies, aquatic insects and smaller dragonflies.

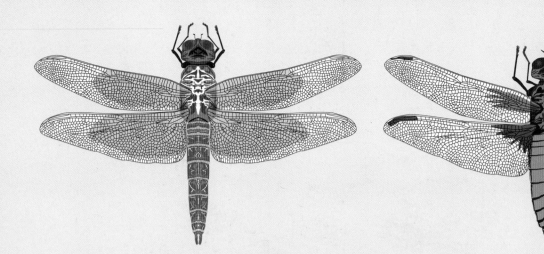

Flame skimmer
Libellula saturata
Wingspan: 85mm

Found across western
North America

This dragonfly favours
warm desert locations
and is usually found near
rivers and hot springs.

Broad-bodied
chaser
Libellula depressa
Length: 45mm

Found across central
and southern Europe,
the Middle East and
central Asia

This medium-sized
dragonfly is fast and
aggressively territorial.
It feeds on small insects
which it catches around
well-vegetated shallow
ponds.

Prince baskettail
Epitheca princeps
Length: 75mm

Found across eastern
North America

This large, highly active
dragonfly often feeds
in swarms, with 10 - 30
individuals congregating
around swamps, ponds
and slow-moving
streams.

Illinois river cruiser
Macromia illinoiensis
Wingspan: 105mm

Found across
North America

This large dragonfly is
found near wide, fast
moving rivers and lakes.

Ebony jewelwing
Calopteryx maculata
Wingspan: 80mm

Found across
North America

This damselfly is usually
found in secluded
streams and small,
plant-rich ponds. It's
a relatively slow flyer
and is quite large for a
damselfly.

FLIES

Flies are a group of insects that make up the order *diptera*. There are around 125,000 known species, although there are estimated to be many more.

True to their name, they are accomplished flyers, with excellent manoeuvrability. Many of them also have very well-developed sensory functions, with good eyesight and efficient smell and taste receptors.

Flies are crucial in the pollination of many flowering plants and in the clearing of waste, making them valuable members of the ecosystem. The larvae (maggots) are efficient consumers of dung, dead animals and dead plant matter.

Bluebottle fly
Calliphora vomitoria
Length: 14mm

Found worldwide

The bluebottle is a very common fly responsible for the spread of some unpleasant illnesses. The adult female lays her eggs on rotting meat and animal waste. Sometimes she can pick up dangerous germs when she does so, and these may spread when she lands on your lunch!

Dark giant horsefly
Tabanus sudeticus
Length: 25mm

Found across Europe

The female of this large biting fly species feeds on the blood of horses, cattle and deer. She also sucks juices from dead, rotting animal carcases.

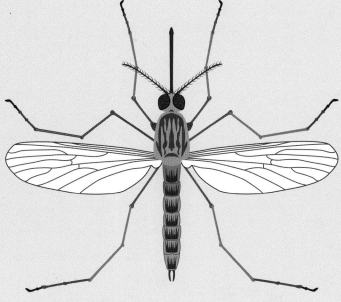

Pied hoverfly
Scaeva pyrastri
Length: 15mm

Found across Europe,
North Africa and Asia

This common hoverfly
feeds on nectar and
pollen, particularly from
bramble flowers.

Common house
mosquito
Culex pipiens
Length: 7mm

Found worldwide

Like many mosquito
species, the blood-
sucking female *Culex
pipiens* can spread
diseases including
meningitis and West Nile
virus.

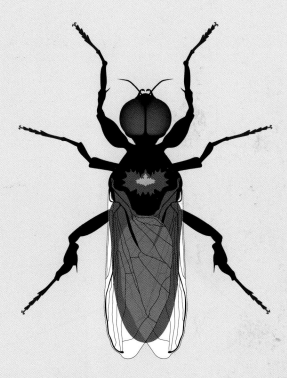

Melon fly
Bactrocera cucurbitae
Length: 8mm

Found across southern
Asia, Africa and Hawaii

The melon fly gets its
name because it is a
major pest, damaging
fruit and vegetable
crops such as melons,
cucumbers and
pumpkins.

St Mark's fly
Bibio marci
Length: 12mm

Found across Europe

The St Mark's fly is often
found around hawthorn
hedgerows and gets its
name because the adults
emerge around St Mark's
Day – 25 April.

MANTIDS, STICK AND LEAF INSECTS

Mantids are members of the order **mantodea**. They are effective predators, with adaptations including accurate eyesight, strong grasping forelegs, and sharp mouthparts. They typically feed on other insects, as well as small reptiles, amphibians and birds.

Stick and leaf insects are members of the order **phasmatodea**. They blend in well with their environment, displaying some of the most impressive camouflage in the animal kingdom. The order contains the longest known insect, the giant Chinese stick insect - *Phryganistria chinensis Zhao.*

Orchid mantis
Hymenopus coronatus
Length: 60mm

Found in tropical southeast Asia

The orchid mantis has evolved an amazing appearance, mimicking tropical orchid flowers. Its appearance means that smaller flying insects approach it, expecting a meal of nectar, and are instead eaten by the mantis.

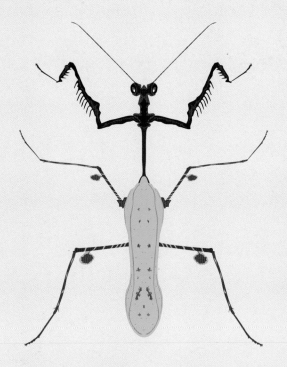

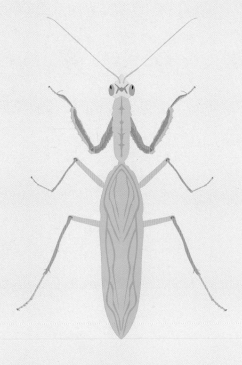

Cryptic mantis
Sibylla pretiosa
Length: 45mm

Found across
southern Africa

The cryptic mantis lives
in forest habitats, on
tree bark, and predates
on smaller flying insects
such as flies and moths.

Giant rainforest
mantis
Hierodula majuscula
Length: 110mm

Found in Australia

This aggressive
predatory mantis feeds
on a wide variety of
other insects, spiders,
and even some small
lizards and amphibians.

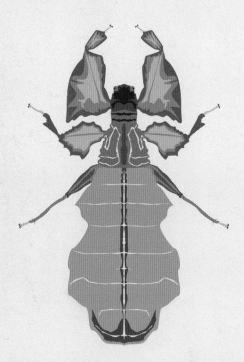

Giant Malaysian
leaf insect
Phyllium giganteum
Length: 95mm

Found in the
Malaysian rainforest

This species is
camouflaged to blend
into its jungle habitat,
and it has even evolved
a swaying walk to mimic
the movement of a leaf
moving in the wind.

Thorny devil
Eurycantha horrida
Length: 130mm

Found in the rainforests
of Papua New Guinea

Unlike most stick insects
which employ camouflage
for defence against
predators, the thorny devil
has sharp spines on its
legs and abdomen which
it uses aggressively to
protect itself.

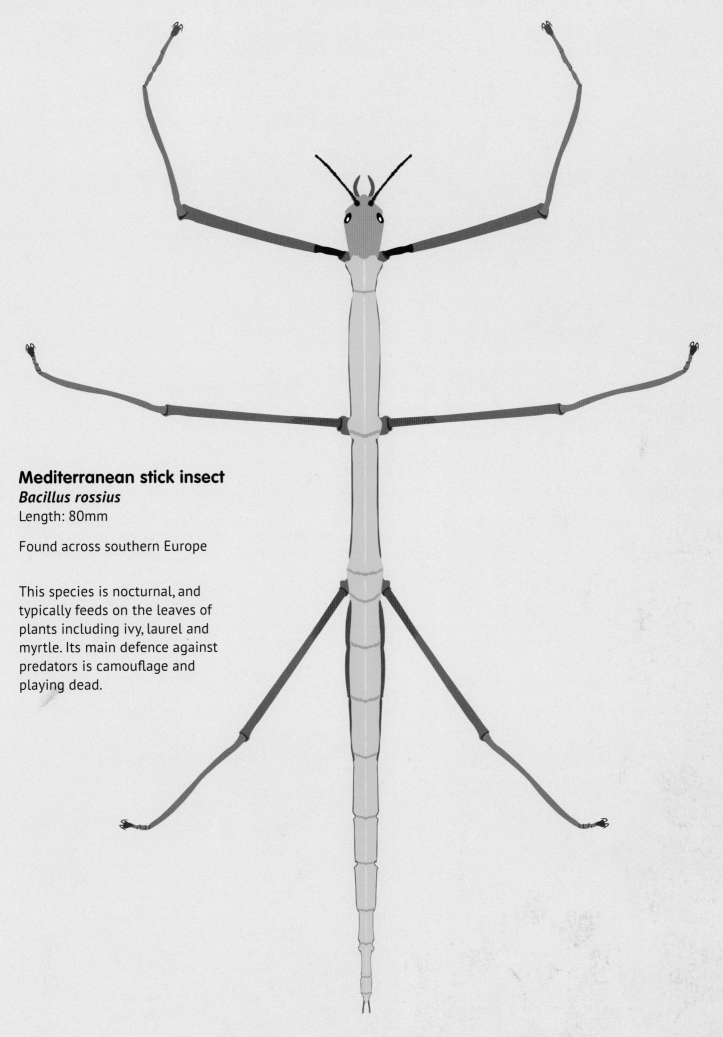

Mediterranean stick insect
Bacillus rossius
Length: 80mm

Found across southern Europe

This species is nocturnal, and typically feeds on the leaves of plants including ivy, laurel and myrtle. Its main defence against predators is camouflage and playing dead.

GRASSHOPPERS, LOCUSTS AND CRICKETS

Grasshoppers, locusts and crickets are members of the order **orthoptera**. They typically have long bodies with large hind legs, which allow them to jump long distances. Some species can produce sounds by rubbing these legs against their wings.

The majority of them are herbivores, and they can cause problems for farmers. Certain species of locust travelling in large swarms are able to wipe out entire crop plantations in a single day.

Rainbow grasshopper
Dactylotum bicolor
Length: 35mm

Found in North America and Mexico

The rainbow grasshopper's bright colour is a defensive adaptation – it functions to mimic other brightly-coloured poisonous bugs so it doesn't get eaten.

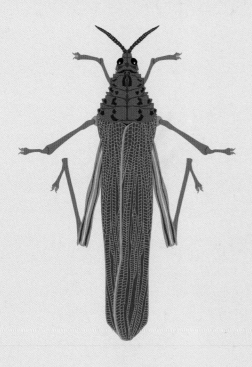

Green milkweed locust
Phymateus viridipes
Length: 70mm

Found across southern Africa

This locust species migrates in huge swarms, travelling for long distances across Africa.

Foaming grasshopper
Dictyophorus spumans
Length: 80mm

Found across Africa

This grasshopper species gets its name because of the toxic foam that it produces in glands in its thorax. It uses this foam to deter potential predators.

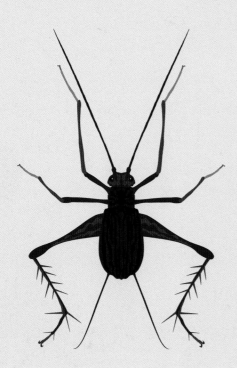

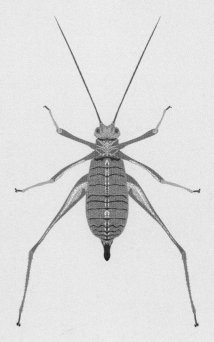

African cave cricket
Speleiacris tabulae
Length: 35mm

Found in central and southern Africa

This species lives in caves and other dark, cool places and feeds on lichen.

Speckled bush-cricket
Leptophyes punctatissima
Length: 16mm

Found across central and southern Europe and the Middle East

This small cricket species is usually found on the edges of woodland areas and in hedgerows.

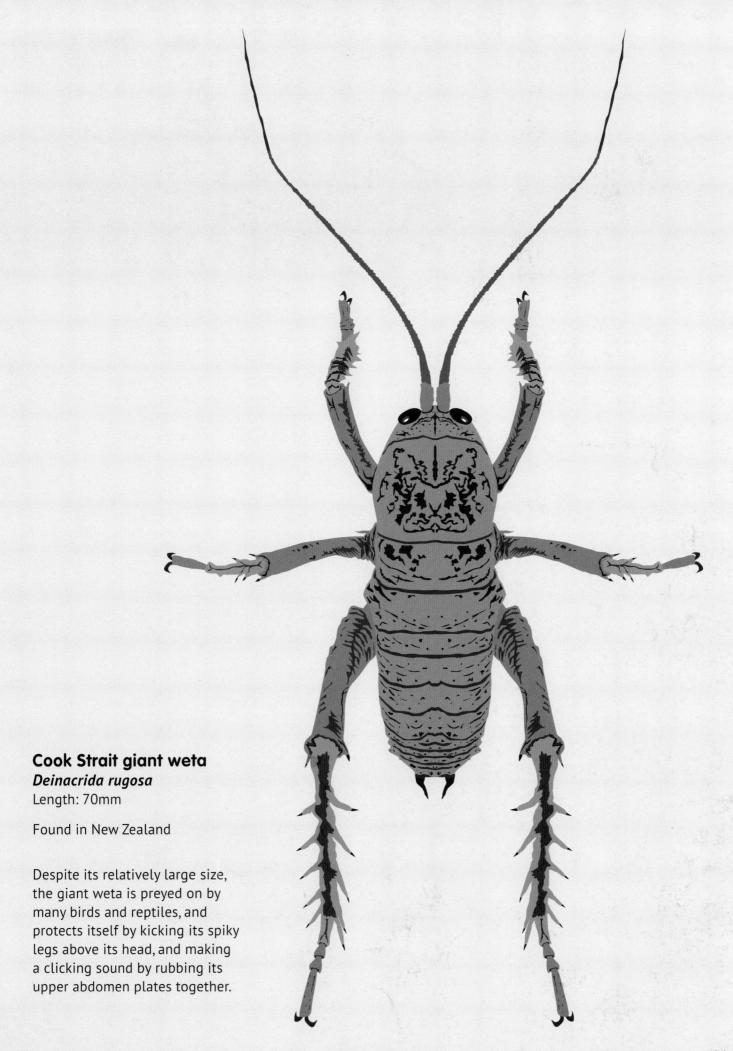

Cook Strait giant weta
Deinacrida rugosa
Length: 70mm

Found in New Zealand

Despite its relatively large size, the giant weta is preyed on by many birds and reptiles, and protects itself by kicking its spiky legs above its head, and making a clicking sound by rubbing its upper abdomen plates together.

COCKROACHES AND TERMITES

Cockroaches and termites are members of the order **blattodea**. The order contains around 8,000 species in total.

Both cockroaches and termites are social insects. Termite society is highly structured; whereas cockroaches have a less sophisticated system, mainly just living and eating together.

Because they like to eat wood, termites can cause serious damage to wood-framed buildings and other wooden structures.

Madagascar hissing cockroach
Gromphadorhina portentosa
Length: 70mm

Found on the African island of Madagascar

This cockroach gets its name because it is able to use an internal sac to force air through the spiracles on its abdomen to produce a characteristic hissing sound.

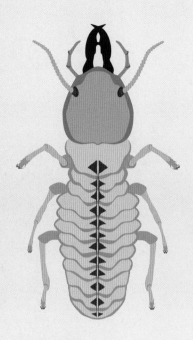

Formosan subterranean termite
Coptotermes formosanus
Length: 5mm

Found in east Asia, South Africa and North America

The Formosan subterranean termite is very destructive, and colonies are able to consume huge quantities of wood material, including timber buildings and boats.

Giant burrowing cockroach
Macropanesthia rhinoceros
Length: 80mm

Found in Australia

The giant burrowing cockroach is the heaviest of its order, and typically feeds on rotting eucalyptus leaves.

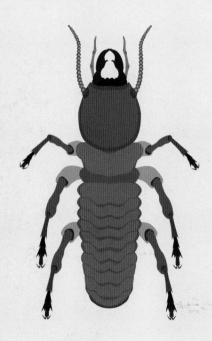

Darwin termite
Mastotermes darwiniensis
Length: 12mm

Found in northern Australia

This primitive species of termite is very similar in appearance to a small cockroach. It nests in tree trunks and stumps.

Smooth cockroach
Symploce pallens
Length: 30mm

Found in the southern USA, Mexico, South America and southeast Asia

This fast-breeding cockroach species has become a problem pest in southeast Asia where it often infests houses, shops and restaurants.

Domino cockroach
Therea petiveriana
Length: 30mm

Found in southern India

The domino cockroach
has evolved to mimic the
appearance of the well-
defended six-spot ground
beetle, which helps it to
avoid the attention
of predators.

THE BIGGEST BUGS AND THE SMALLEST BUGS

Just as bugs show a huge range of diversity in colour, shape and pattern, they are also found in a very wide range of sizes.

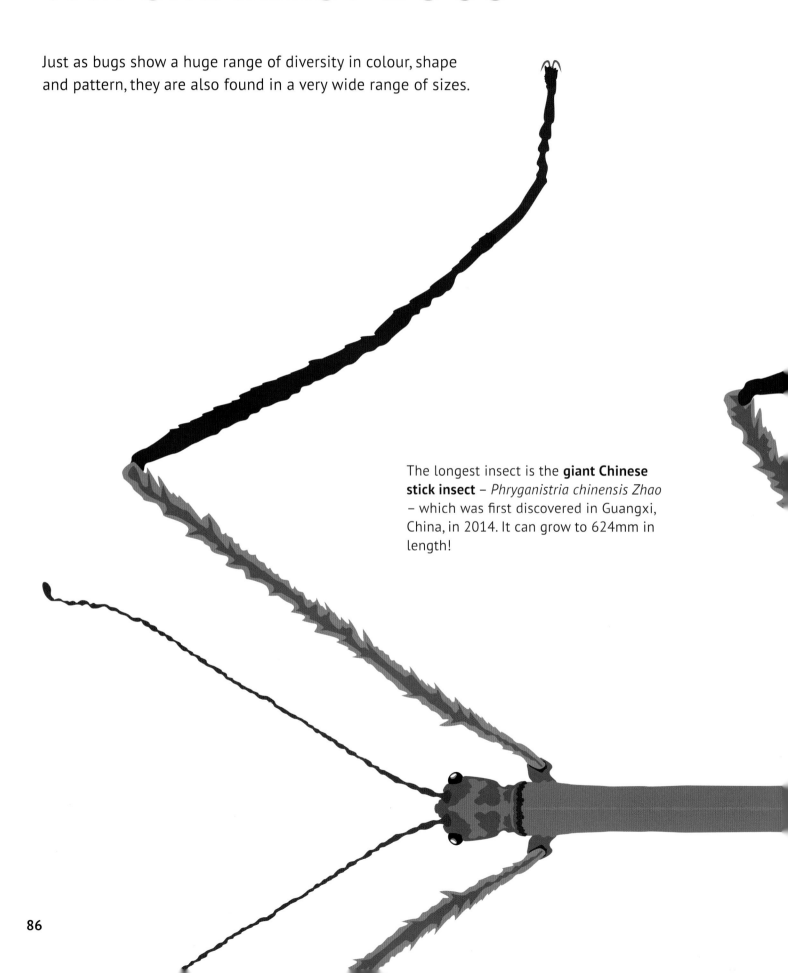

The longest insect is the **giant Chinese stick insect** – *Phryganistria chinensis Zhao* – which was first discovered in Guangxi, China, in 2014. It can grow to 624mm in length!

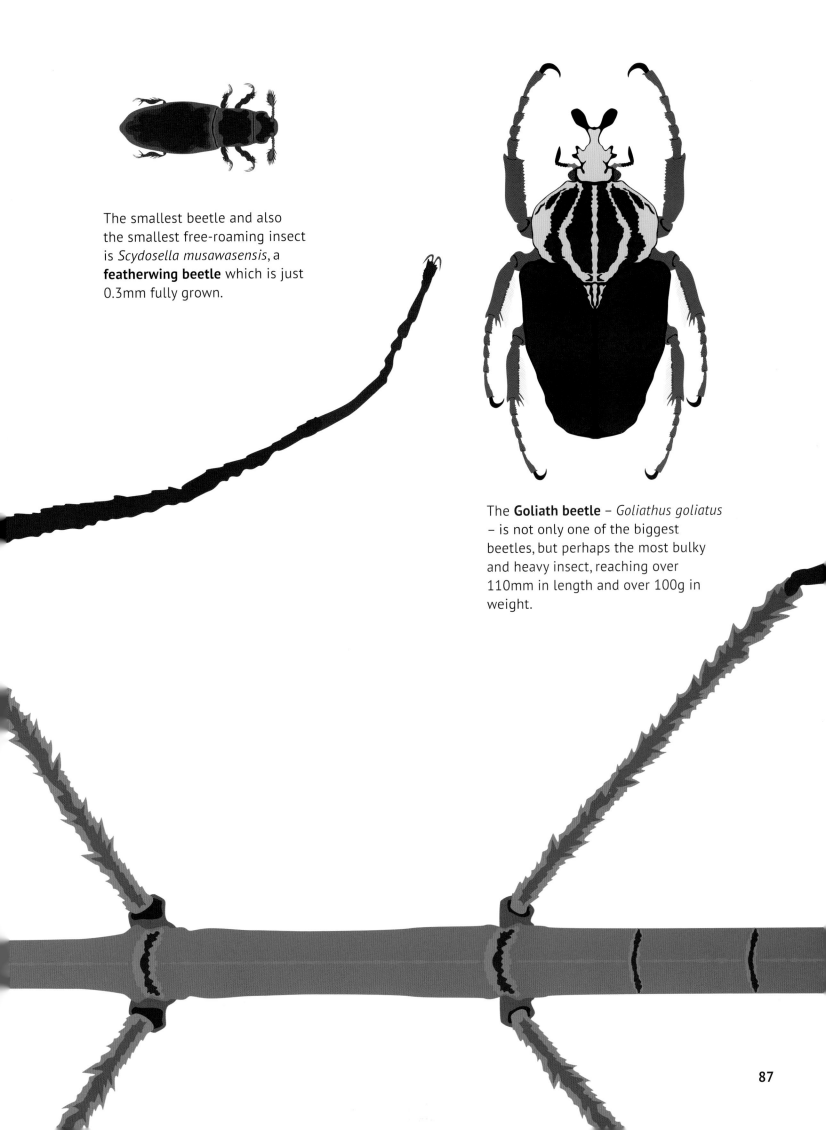

The smallest beetle and also the smallest free-roaming insect is *Scydosella musawasensis*, a **featherwing beetle** which is just 0.3mm fully grown.

The **Goliath beetle** – *Goliathus goliatus* – is not only one of the biggest beetles, but perhaps the most bulky and heavy insect, reaching over 110mm in length and over 100g in weight.

The smallest butterfly is the **western pygmy blue** – *Brephidium exilis* – which has a wingspan of just 12mm!

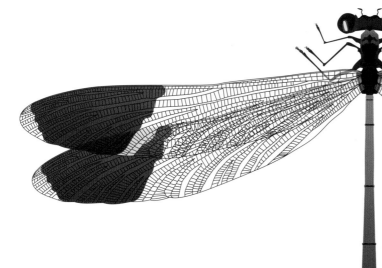

The largest insect in the dragonfly and damselfly order is the **helicopter damselfly** – *Megaloprepus caerulatus* – which has a wingspan of up to 190mm.

The largest ant is the queen **driver ant** – *Dorylus helvolus* – which can reach a massive 80mm in length.

The biggest butterfly is the **Queen Alexandra's birdwing** – *Ornithoptera alexandrae* – which can reach a wingspan of over 250mm.

The largest fly is the **mydas fly** – *Gauromydas heros* – which has a wingspan of 100mm.

THE MOST DANGEROUS BUGS

Despite their small size, some insects can be very dangerous. The deadliest bug in the world isn't itself poisonous at all, but it carries a very serious disease that kills hundreds of thousands of people every year. This bug carries malaria, and is the **anopheles mosquito** – *Anopheles gambiae*. Malaria is an infectious disease found in a broad band around the Equator, where it is caused by tiny organisms called **PROTOZOA** that are carried by the female anopheles mosquito. They don't make the mosquito ill at all. Organisms that transmit diseases in this way are called **VECTORS**.

The mosquito feeds by landing on a larger animal, sticking its long, sharp proboscis into the animal's skin. The proboscis tip is like a needle, and the mosquito feels around for a blood vessel. When it locates one, it plunges the proboscis into it.

Before the mosquito starts sucking the blood out, it injects saliva into its target. The saliva does various jobs. Most importantly it stops the blood clotting while the mosquito is feeding.
It is the saliva that causes raised mosquito bite bumps. In infected mosquitoes, it is the saliva that carries malaria, and the saliva injection is what transmits the malaria disease.

Male mosquitoes can get enough nutrients from nectar and other juices from plants. Female mosquitoes require extra nutrients, including proteins, in order to develop eggs. This is why they need to feed on animal (or human) blood. Other types of mosquito can carry diseases in this way, but only the anopheles mosquito can carry malaria.

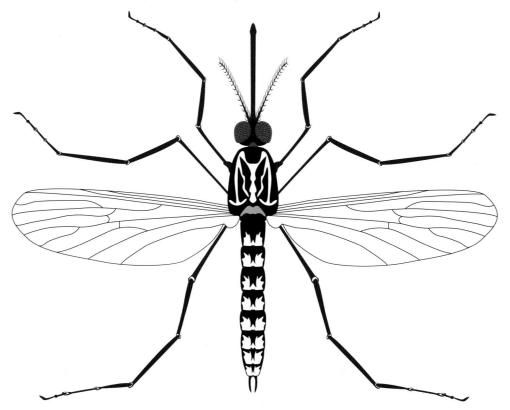

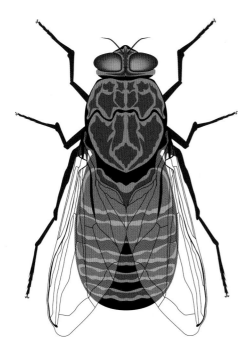

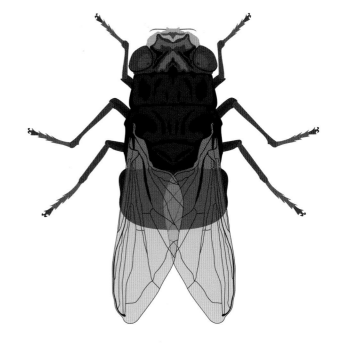

The **tsetse fly** – *Glossina palpalis* – is also a vector, and can transmit a disease called trypanosomiasis, commonly known as sleeping sickness. This is a very serious disease that is hard to treat, and it kills many people in central Africa.

Found in South and Central America, the female **human botfly** – *Dermatobia hominis* – catches and lays her eggs on a mosquito. When the mosquito is feeding on a human, the eggs are transferred and start developing into a larva inside the skin of their host. They then hatch out of the skin before pupating into an adult botfly. The hatch sites can become infected, and infestation of the brain has caused death in children.

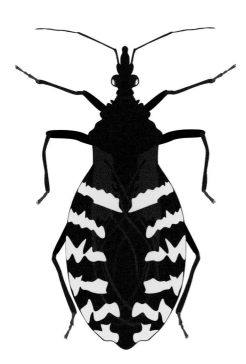

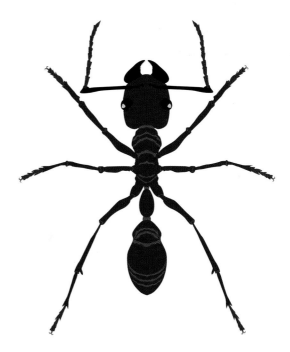

The **assassin bug** – *Triatoma infestans* – carries the protozoa responsible for the tropical Chagas disease. The bug can transmit this when it feeds by biting and sucking blood from humans. There is no vaccine to protect against the disease, and it can lead to serious heart damage.

The South and Central American **bullet ant** – *Paraponera clavata* – has the most potent sting of any insect. The chemical in its sting is known as a **NEUROTOXIN,** and it causes extreme pain as well as swelling and paralysis.

BENEFICIAL BUGS

Many different types of bugs perform services that are beneficial for the ecosystem as a whole, and for humans in particular. Thousands of plant species rely on bugs to spread pollen to help them reproduce – those vitally important bugs include bees, flies, wasps, butterflies, moths and ants. Other bugs, such as ladybirds and hoverflies, feed on small insects that would otherwise destroy crops.

Ground beetles eat slugs and snails, dung beetles deal with animal waste, and many beetle and fly larvae consume dead or decaying plant material.

Plants have evolved bright colours and nectar-secreting glands to attract bugs, because they are so important to their existence. We should always remember how important they are to ours too.

The **western honey bee** – *Apis mellifera* – is the main species of domesticated bee, used for the production of honey. This species is also extremely important for crop pollination, with all sorts of fruit and vegetable plants relying on them for this service.

The **sacred scarab beetle** – *Scarabaeus sacer* – is a type of dung beetle found in southern Europe, the Middle East and North Africa. Dung beetles eat, move and bury animal waste, which benefits other animals, and also improves the nutrient levels and structure of the soil.

Ancient Egyptians saw sacred scarab beetles rolling balls of dung to their nest burrows, and so believed that the sun must be rolled across the sky by a scarab god!

The **seven-spot ladybird** – *Coccinella septempunctata* – is the most common ladybird in the UK. Both the adult ladybird and its larvae are voracious consumers of aphids. This in turn protects delicate young plants from aphid damage, which is why ladybirds are popular with gardeners!

GLOSSARY

ABDOMEN The third section of the bug's body, containing the heart, the final section of the guts, the reproductive organs and the sting

ANAUTOGENY The requirement of some female bugs to consume blood before they are able to produce eggs

ANTENNAE Sensory organs that bugs use to detect smell, heat, wind and vibrations, and can also use as feelers

APHID Small true bugs that are plant pests

ARTHROPOD The largest animal phylum, arthropods are invertebrates with an exoskeleton and jointed legs

BINOMIAL Double-named system for naming species

CARNIVOROUS Meat-eating

CERCI Appendages at the rear of certain insects. Can be sensory, defensive or a vestigial structure

CHARACTERISTICS Defining features

CHITIN The strong protein that makes up insect exoskeleton and wings

CLASS Larger set in taxonomy e.g. *insecta* (insects)

COLONY A eusocial community

COMPOUND EYES Complex eyes with lots of separate lenses

EUSOCIAL A complex arrangement of living together and dividing labour

EXOSKELETON Hard outer skeleton

FAMILY Large set in taxonomy e.g. *formicidae* (ants)

FERTILE Having the ability to breed (have children)

GENUS A small set in taxonomy; the first half of the species name e.g. *Myrmecia* (bull ants)

HAEMOLYMPH A fluid similar to blood that transports nutrients and oxygen around the body

HEAD CAPSULE A hard structure containing the brain, mouthparts and sensory organs

HEXAPOD A set of arthropods with six legs

IMAGO The final (or adult) stage in the lifecycle of an insect

INVERTEBRATES A group of animals with no backbone

LABIUM The lower part of the front of an insect's mouth

LARVA The second life stage of some insects, following the egg stage

MANDIBLES A pair of mouthparts that can be used to hold, cut or chew the insect's food. Some insects (such as stag beetles) have very large mandibles, which they use for fighting

MAXILLARY PALPS A pair of appendages that certain bugs use for moving food towards the mouth

METAMORPHOSIS The transition of an insect from one life stage to another

NEUROTOXIN A powerful chemical found in certain bug stings that affects the nervous system of the creature (or person) stung by the bug

NYMPH A form of the larval stage of certain insects in which the insect looks like a smaller version of the adult

OCELLI A simple insect eye with just one lens

OLFACTORY RECEPTOR An apparatus that certain bugs use to smell and taste things, particularly food

OMMATIDIA The individual units that make up the compound eye

ORDER Larger set in taxonomy e.g. *hymenoptera* (bees, wasps and ants)

ORGANISM A living being, such as an animal, a plant or a bacterium

PATHOGEN A microorganism that causes disease

PHYLUM Large set in taxonomy e.g. *arthropoda* (arthropods)

PREDATOR An animal that preys on/eats others

PROBOSCIS An elongated tubular mouthpart used by certain bugs for feeding

PROTOZOA Tiny single-celled organisms

PUPA The life stage of an insect in between larva and imago. Not all insects go through the pupa stage

SIPHONING An eating technique used by bugs using a proboscis

SPECIES The smallest set of taxonomy e.g. *Myrmecia gulosa* (red bull ant)

TAXONOMY How scientists group organisms into sets

THORAX The second section of the bug's body, which contains the first section of the bug's gut and circulatory system. The legs and wings (if present) are attached to the exterior of the thorax

TYMPANEL ORGANS Hearing apparatus, rather like a drum, with a thin membrane that vibrates when exposed to sound

VECTOR An organism that carries an infectious pathogen without being affected by the disease itself

VESTIGIAL STRUCTURE A part of a bug's anatomy which is genetically inherited but no longer serves any useful function

To my parents, Michael and Diana

First published in the United Kingdom in 2017 by
Pavilion Children's Books
43 Great Ormond Street
London
WC1N 3HZ

An imprint of Pavilion Books Limited.

Publisher and Editor: Neil Dunnicliffe
Art Director: Lee-May Lim

Text and illustrations © Simon Tyler 2017
Bug Consultant: Rory Dimond, Buglife

The moral rights of the author and illustrator have been asserted

ISBN: 9781843653431

A CIP catalogue record for this book is available from the British Library.

10 9 8 7 6 5 4 3 2 1

Reproduction by Rival Colour UK
Printed by Toppan Leefung Printing Ltd, China

This book can be ordered directly from the publisher online
at www.pavilionbooks.com, or try your local bookshop.